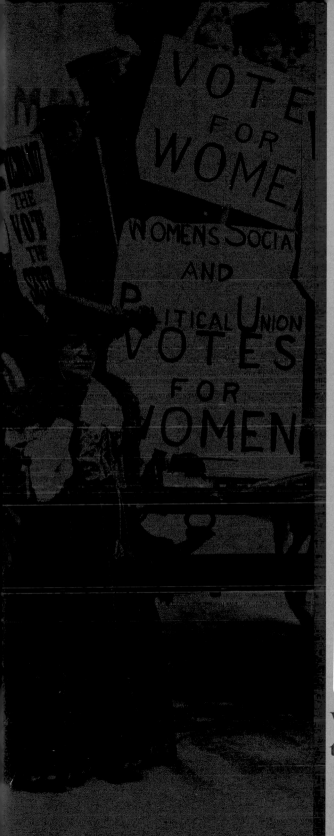

Women's Right to Vote

PERSPECTIVES ON

Women's Right to Vote

America's Suffrage Movement

KATIE MARSICO

Marshall Cavendish
Benchmark

New York

This publication represents the opinions and views of the author based on Katie Marsico's personal experience, knowledge, and research. The information in this book serves as a general guide only. The author and publisher have used their best efforts in preparing this book and disclaim liability rising directly and indirectly from the use and application of this book.

Other Marshall Cavendish Offices: Marshall Cavendish International (Asia) Private Limited, 1 New Industrial Road, Singapore 536196 • Marshall Cavendish International (Thailand) Co Ltd. 253 Asoke, 12th Flr, Sukhumvit 21 Road, Klongtoey Nua, Wattana, Bangkok 10110, Thailand • Marshall Cavendish (Malaysia) Sdn Bhd, Times Subang, Lot 46, Subang Hi-Tech Industrial Park, Batu Tiga, 40000 Shah Alam, Selangor Darul Ehsan, Malaysia

Marshall Cavendish is a trademark of Times Publishing Limited

All websites were available and accurate when this book was sent to press.

Library of Congress Cataloging-in-Publication Data

Marsico, Katie, 1980–
Women's right to vote : America's suffrage movement / by Katie Marsico.
p. cm. — (Perspectives on)
Includes bibliographical references and index.
Summary: "Provides comprehensive information on the suffrage movement in the United States and differing perspectives accompanying it" — Provided by publisher.
ISBN 978-0-7614-4980-5
1. Women—Suffrage—United States—History. I. Title.
JK1896.M385 2010
324.6'230973—dc22
2009030925

Editor: Christine Florie
Publisher: Michelle Bisson
Art Director: Anahid Hamparian
Series Designer: Sonia Chaghatzbanian

Expert Reader: Sally Roesch Wagner, Executive Director, The Matilda Joslyn Gage Center, Fayetteville, New York

Photo research by Marybeth Kavanagh

Cover photo by Topham/The Image Works

The photographs in this book are used by permission and through the courtesy of: *Alamy*: North Wind Picture Archives, 2–3; Mary Evans Picture Library, 49; Jeff Greenberg, 83; *Corbis*: Bettmann, 8, 19, 28, 43, 62, 67; Underwood & Underwood, 35; *Getty Images*: Cincinnati Museum Center, 11; Stock Montage, 59; HASSAN AMMAR/AFP, 73; George Frey, 75 (left); Sara D. Davis, 75 (right); *The Granger Collection, NY*: 17, 21, 38; *Photoedit*: Michael Ventura, 30; *The Image Works*: akg-images, 47

Printed in Malaysia (T)
1 3 5 6 4 2

Contents

Introduction

THE IDEA THAT WOMEN SHOULD BE ACCORDED the right to vote — a right technically referred to as suffrage or the franchise — was at the center of much heated debate and national controversy from the 1840s onward. Suffragists — those who favored and fought for this idea — believed that all U.S. citizens, regardless of gender, should be able to cast a ballot and campaigned for a constitutional amendment to achieve this end.

In the early twentieth century, when the proposed amendment came under the greatest scrutiny, suffragists insisted that women possessed the intelligence and political awareness to make informed decisions at the polls, despite the limited opportunities in education and career advancement that society then afforded them. The suffragists' triumph came in 1920, with the ratification of the Nineteenth Amendment to the U.S. Constitution.

Many men — even some antisuffragist women — opposed the amendment on the basis of everything from religious principles to social order. Women, they argued, helped maintain society's stability by providing tranquillity and order in the domestic sphere. Did they truly want to enter the political arena, which was foreign to the kitchen, the parlor, and the nursery, the domains to which women were accustomed?

Congressional discussion of the amendment intensified in the years after 1910, the period during which first Europe and then the United States became embroiled in World War I (1914–1918). Some opponents of suffrage, arguing that a squabble over the vote for women was inappropriate in time of war, cautioned Americans not to disrupt a social system in which women and men had clearly designated roles.

From the standpoint of the present, the end of the first decade of the twenty-first century, a comprehensive view of all the perspectives related to the passage of the Nineteenth Amendment is not a simple matter. Many people could find it hard to grasp why suffragists led hunger strikes from their jail cells in 1917 or why certain prominent male politicians were determined to keep women away from the ballot box. One needs to understand the differing opinions of those who favored and opposed the constitutional change, as well as the specific concerns of those who had to grapple with the problems of enforcing the amendment in the decades after its ratification. Without this understanding, today's voters can hardly appreciate what the presence of both genders at the polls means in historical, social, and political terms.

One

A Woman's Voice in a Man's World

CARRIE CHAPMAN CATT, a leader in the women's suffrage movement, delivered a speech titled "The Crisis" on September 7, 1916, in Atlantic City, New Jersey, at a convention in support of women's voting rights. The convention's atmosphere was charged by the belief that America's political system was in need of immediate change. Indeed, with the Great War (World War I) soon to include the United States among the combatants, a formidable national crisis was inevitable.

In the nineteenth century, Catt and other like-minded women began waging a difficult battle that they hoped would win women a voice in national affairs. After all, they argued, America had never been a nation of men alone. Though women admittedly enjoyed few career and educational opportunities outside the home, they had nonetheless played a critical part in supporting their country from the moment of its inception in the late 1700s.

From the earliest days, American women—mothers, wives, and sisters—had raised families and run households

As a new century dawned, some women spoke out for their rights. A suffragist addresses her peers in 1914 at a suffrage gathering in Newport, Rhode Island.

during periods of war and hardship, as well as during peaceful and prosperous times. Other women had labored in classrooms, hospitals, and town meeting halls; by the early twentieth century, many of them felt entitled to have a voice in local and national elections. A select few had reached the White House as first lady, and several first ladies had been extremely influential. As taxpaying citizens of a republic, ever more women began to insist that they had a right to full participation in the political sphere. Since the end of the Civil War, women had seen the right to vote extended to virtually every segment of the population except for themselves. This fact alone galvanized the suffrage movement, no matter what opposition it faced.

In the autumn of 1916, the United States was on the brink of entering World War I. Even when national attention was not completely focused on impending war, opponents of the suffrage movement put forth the age-old argument that a woman's place was in the domestic sphere, unburdened by political matters and defined by the leadership of fathers, husbands, and brothers. From the perspective of many average citizens and several notable politicians, with the country so close to war, it was more crucial than ever that this stability be maintained on the home front.

Such were the opinions and international tensions that swirled around the suffragists who awaited Catt's words in the fall of 1916. For her part, the suffrage leader was aware that, regardless of whatever outside chaos and opposition threatened to envelope their movement, those citizens who supported a woman's right to vote needed to remain firm in their convictions and dedicated to their cause. Catt challenged her followers:

If you believe with me that a crisis has come
to our movement, if you believe that the
time for final action is now, if you catch the
rosy tints of the coming day, what does it
mean to you? Does it not give you a thrill
of exaltation; does the blood not course
more quickly through your veins; does it not
bring a new sense of freedom, of joy, and of
determination? Is it not true that you who
wanted a little time ago to lay down the work
because you were weary with long service,
now, under the compelling influence of a

Carrie Chapman Catt became involved in women's suffrage in the late 1800s
and later became a leader in the U.S. suffrage movement.

changed mental attitude, are ready to go
on until the vote is won? The change is one
of spirit! Aye, and the spiritual effect upon
you will come to others. . . . What our great
movement needs now is a "mobilization of
spirit"—the jubilant, glad spirit of victory.
Then let us sound a bugle call here and now
to the women of the nation: "The woman's
hour has struck." Let the bugle sound from
the suffrage headquarters of every state at
the inauguration of a state campaign. Let
the call go forth again and again and yet
again. Let it be repeated in every article
written, in every speech made, in every
conversation held. Let the bugle blow again
and yet again. The political emancipation
of our sex call[s] you, women of America,
arise! Are you content that others shall pay
the price of your liberty? Women in schools
and counting house, in shops and on the
farm, women in the home with babes at
their breasts, and women engaged in public
careers will hear. The veins of American
women are not filled with milk and water.
They are neither cowards nor slackers. They
will come. They only await the bugle call to
learn that the final battle is on.

As Catt correctly surmised, the battle was indeed on. Emerg-
ing from it victorious, however, would entail addressing a
multitude of often varying perspectives on the issue of suffrage.

Ultimately, victory was sealed with the ratification of the Nineteenth Amendment to the U.S. Constitution.

A Set Role in Society

Women had contributed to the welfare and vitality of the United States even before independence, primarily as homemakers and caretakers. For hundreds of years, members of the so-called gentler sex were expected to submit to the will and control of their male counterparts on the basis of deeply rooted social and religious values. In the eighteenth and nineteenth centuries, most women were taught to value marriage into a prestigious family and raising children far more than an advanced education, which was sometimes even considered a liability. The British author John Gregory even went so far as to advise young women that "if you happen to have any learning, keep it a profound secret."

Everyone from scholars to church leaders argued that a docile, soft-spoken young lady who submitted to the men in her life was the model of all that was natural and intended by God. Theological experts pointed to biblical portrayals of women such as Eve that fit this prototype and argued that famous New Testament figures such as Saint Paul had taken issue with females who spoke during church gatherings. It was far better, many men — and even some women — continued to conclude more than a millennium later, for ladies to keep silent and let their superiors do the majority of the decision making at home, in business, and at the forefront of politics. From their perspective, the notion of altering the status quo was both radical and unnecessary. Women who ultimately came to oppose suffrage in the United States, including Madeleine V. Dahlgren, Ellen Boyle Ewing Sherman, and Almira

Remember the Ladies . . .

As early as 1776, future First Lady Abigail Adams, whose husband—John Adams—served as the U.S. president from 1797 to 1801, recognized the importance of giving female citizens a voice in politics. Addressing her husband during his service in the Continental Congress, she requested, "In the new code of laws [that] I suppose it will be necessary for you to make, I desire you would remember the ladies and be more generous and favorable to them than your ancestors." In her role as first lady, Adams became renowned for advising the president on national affairs and for the high regard in which he held her perspectives.

Hart Lincoln Phelps, listed the following specific reasons for their argument against such social changes in the late 1800s:

> Because Holy Scripture inculcates a different and, for us, a higher sphere apart from public life. Because, as women, we find a full measure of duties and responsibilities devolving upon us, and we are therefore unwilling to bear other and heavier burdens and those unsuited to our physical organization. . . . Because these changes must introduce a fruitful element of discord in the existing marriage relation, which would tend to the detriment of children and increase the already alarming prevalence of divorce throughout the land. Because no general law affecting the condition of all women should be framed to meet exceptional discontent.

These women and others like them subscribed to the notion that girls were reared to be obedient daughters, dutiful wives, and patient mothers. Skills such as sewing, cooking, and cleaning were considered assets, and any additional knowledge was generally of value only so long as it could be imparted to the children in a woman's care. Until the 1830s, women had few opportunities to pursue a college degree, and most careers outside of teaching, nursing, or clerical or domestic positions were closed to them.

Ultimately, women began to voice their objections to their designated lot in life. Several early champions of women's rights emerged from the Quaker religion and the

Early in American history, married women did not merely take their husband's name when they wed. For all intents and purposes, a man owned his spouse and all of their children and any property in his bride's possession. If he decided to beat his family or send them to a workhouse where the poor were forced into labor, they had little recourse to object. Women did gain greater control over their holdings and basic rights during the nineteenth century, but unlike today, divorce settlements tended to favor the husband until well into the 1900s.

Early American society expected women to remain in the home as family caregivers and homemakers.

abolitionist movement. Quakers generally upheld the belief that men and women shared equality before God and should therefore maintain similar rights on Earth. Most abolitionists, whose aim was to end slavery in America, were unconcerned about female suffrage or plainly opposed to it.

Women who spoke out to eradicate slavery were often regarded suspiciously and condescendingly by their male counterparts. While most of these men did not doubt the good intentions of abolitionists such as Sarah and Angelina Grimké, Abby Kelly Foster, Lucretia Mott, Susan B. Anthony, and

Elizabeth Cady Stanton, they were concerned that their frequently boisterous presence would cost the movement's antislavery efforts support. Since far more Americans were interested in slavery than women's rights, ladies in frocks and petticoats raising an uproar at conventions and rallies did the antislavery cause more harm than good.

Sensing this gender divide even among those men who were supposed to be their political comrades, Mott and Stanton took action by organizing the Seneca Falls Convention in July 1848. The meeting, which is now seen as the onset of the women's rights movement, was called to address the social status of America women. The convention issued what it called a Declaration of Sentiments; the document, modeled on the Declaration of Independence, spoke to issues that were specific to women. It began with the statement, "We hold these truths to be self-evident: that all men and women are created equal. . . ."

In keeping with these ideals, suffragists fought to win the same social, legal, and economic opportunities as men, to be held to similar moral standards, and to be given the right to vote. This last goal would prove particularly controversial in the years ahead, especially as, after slavery was legally abolished in 1865, African-American men were granted suffrage with the passage of the Fifteenth Amendment in 1870. The fact that women of both races continued to be denied such a freedom was both a shock and somewhat of an insult to the suffragists.

As Anthony pleaded, "I beg you to speak of woman as you do of the Negro; speak of her as a human being, as a citizen of the United States, as a half of the people in whose hands lies the destiny of this nation." Indeed, Anthony,

Elizabeth Cady Stanton speaks at the first women's rights convention in Seneca Falls, New York, in 1848.

Stanton, and other U.S. suffragists began to rally their forces in the last half of the nineteenth century to organize efforts that would allow female citizens a far greater voice in determining America's destiny.

The First Stages of the Fight for the Vote

Anthony and Stanton joined with others in forming the National Woman Suffrage Association (NWSA) in 1869 to further their ambitions of securing equal rights for American women. Lucy Stone, Henry Blackwell, and Julia Ward Howe created the American Woman Suffrage Association (AWSA) that same year. AWSA focused primarily on voting privileges, whereas NWSA also addressed improved opportunities for females in other areas, including education and employment. Even before such groups took shape, many women had begun to perceive the need to pool their efforts to promote suffrage legislation on a national scale. Consequently, Anthony and her cohorts petitioned the U.S. Congress in 1866 for a constitutional amendment that would address female voting rights.

"In making the demand for suffrage," their formal written request read, "we would call your attention to the fact that we represent 15 million people—one half the entire population of the country—intelligent, virtuous, native-born American citizens; and yet [we] stand outside the pale of political recognition." Referring to themselves as the "only remaining class of disenfranchised citizens," Stanton, Anthony, Stone, and other petitioners pleaded with congressmen to "fulfill [their] constitutional obligation 'to guarantee to every state in the union a republican form of government.'"

Bolstering the suffragists' argument was the fact that legislators in several U.S. territories and states in the West were granting women the right to vote in the last half of the nineteenth century. Politicians in Wyoming, Utah, Colorado, and Idaho largely lent their support to the suffrage movement during the late 1800s. In the Midwest, South, and Northeast, legislators were generally more reluctant. The greater sympathy to female suffrage in the "uncivilized" West struck many as ironic.

Women living along the frontier played a somewhat different social role from those residing in more settled areas. The West's social fluidity gave women greater opportunities to participate in political affairs. Women who dwelled in the Midwest, South, and Northeast were restricted by social structures that had been in place for decades.

This cartoon depicts suffrage as a woman holding a torch and making her way from the western half of the country toward the East.

From the perspective of many politicians and public figures in these regions, the idea of granting females the vote symbolized a disruption to the American way of life as they knew it. For example, Kansas Democrats at an 1894 convention bitterly noted that suffrage would "destroy the home and family." Samuel Clemens—better known as Mark Twain—was equally as forthright in arguing that women should be kept away from the polls. "Women, go your ways," he commanded in a letter he wrote to the St. Louis *Missouri Democrat* in the late 1800s. "Seek not to beguile us of our imperial privileges. Content yourself with your little feminine trifles—your babies, your benevolent societies and your knitting—and let your natural bosses do the voting. Stand back—you will be wanting to go to war next. We will let you teach school as much as you want to, and we will pay you half wages for it, too, but beware! We don't want you to crowd us too much." Ultimately, though, he reversed his opinion.

From the vantage point of certain individuals who supported early suffrage efforts in the last half of the nineteenth century, women voters had a calming and constructive influence on the country. After leaders in Wyoming Territory invited ladies to step up to the ballot box starting in 1869, national suffragists were quick to claim that "the vote of women transformed Wyoming from barbarism to civilization." Several leaders of the suffrage movement during this period were also quick to add that granting women the vote was crucial because females—just like their male counterparts—were members of American civilization who were affected by many of the same day-to-day conflicts and issues that found resolution in U.S. politics.

"The talk of sheltering woman from the fierce storms of life is the sheerest mockery, for they beat on her from every point of the compass, just as they do on man, and with more fatal results, for he has been trained to protect himself, to resist, to conquer," explained Stanton in 1892. "Such are the facts in human experience, the responsibilities of individual sovereignty. Rich and poor, intelligent and ignorant, wise and foolish, virtuous and vicious, man and woman, it is ever the same, each soul must depend wholly on itself." At the beginning of the twentieth century, it began to become clear that the individuality Stanton referred to was an extremely powerful force within the suffrage movement. The presence of leaders with different ideas and attitudes led to undeniable conflicts and controversies that divided suffragists just as the push to pass a constitutional amendment gained momentum.

Two

Opposing Opinions on Achieving Suffrage

THOUGH CONGRESS REPEATEDLY REFUSED to pass legislation that would enable women to vote in national elections, suffragists continued to press hard to promote their cause during the final decades of the nineteenth century. Although they succeeded in helping women across America win the right to cast a ballot in local and school board elections, the goal of enfranchising all female citizens required a constitutional amendment.

Critics of suffrage undermined this steadfast determination by pointing to the discord that was already evident among women fighting for the vote. The differing philosophies of AWSA and NWSA had resulted in a nonunified front on the part of the suffragists. It was also obvious that there was debate on the extent to which racial and ethnic questions should be addressed.

Famous African Americans such as Ida B. Wells-Barnett and Sojourner Truth favored voting rights for women, but their presence in the movement was not always universally appreciated by their fellow activists. Just as male abolitionists had decried the efforts of their female counterparts on the basis of their gender detracting from their cause, so did certain white, U.S.-born suffragists frown on immigrants and women from other races joining their ranks. In some cases, racial and cultural discrimination was at the root of their disapproval.

In other situations, though, supporters of women's suffrage were worried that a person's skin color or country of origin would prevent politicians from perceiving a constitutional amendment as benefiting an educated and established group of people. They feared congressmen would resist putting presidential elections in the hands of women who came from distant lands or who earned meager wages as cooks and maids. Even the well-known suffragist Carrie Chapman Catt publicly condemned "aggressive movements that with possibly ill-advised haste [have] enfranchised the foreigner, the Negro, and the Indian." Women from these backgrounds, however, felt that they needed to win the vote more than anyone else.

"If white American women, with all their natural advantages need the ballot," observed the prominent African-American suffragist Adele Hunt Logan, "how much more do black Americans, male and female, need the strong defense of the vote to help secure their right to life, liberty, and the pursuit of happiness?" Internal debates that arose within the suffrage movement over this issue and others continued to give the impression of a divided front. This in turn only seemed to detract from the efforts of activists in the eyes of both the general public and the politicians who wielded power in Washington, D.C.

In an attempt to further strengthen the suffrage movement, NWSA and AWSA united in 1890 and formed the National American Woman Suffrage Association (NAWSA); the newly united group worked toward the goal of winning the vote on a state-by-state basis. Members of NAWSA reasoned that if a majority of states passed legislation in their

America: Not the First

The United States was not the first country to grant suffrage to women. Other nations such as Sweden, Australia, the Pitcairn Islands, the United Kingdom, Canada, New Zealand, Finland, Denmark, Norway, Azerbaijan, Austria, Estonia, Germany, Latvia, Poland, the Russian Federation, Armenia, Belarus, Belgium, Georgia, Hungary, Luxembourg, the Netherlands, the Ukraine, Albania, and the former Czechoslovakia each extended this right to their female residents on some level prior to the passage of the Nineteenth Amendment. As of 1920, however, many countries still imposed voting restrictions or limited female participation in political affairs.

favor, then Congress would have no choice but to consider an amendment to the U.S. Constitution.

Another Split and a New President

Politicians in Washington, D.C., for the most part continued to ignore the possibility of such legislation during the early 1900s. Suffragists had nonetheless realized success as a result of their efforts during this period. Little by little, additional states, including Washington, Oregon, California, Kansas, and Arizona, started acknowledging that women should have the right to vote. In addition, Catt, who acted as president of NAWSA from 1900 through 1904, instituted suffrage schools, which instructed students in the background of the movement, the best ways to bolster membership in the organization, and tactics for convincing people from all walks of life that enfranchising women was in the best interest of the country.

Not everyone agreed that NAWSA was acting fast enough or with sufficient effectiveness. Prosuffrage critics of the group questioned the zeal of activists who politely lobbied in Washington, D.C., and who maintained hope that state-by-state legislation would ultimately prove the answer to their endeavors. Harriot Stanton Blatch, daughter of Elizabeth Cady Stanton, was among the suffragists who took exception to this approach. Forming what eventually became known as the Women's Political Union (WPU) in 1910, she utilized aggressive techniques that included picketing at open-air gatherings, and a parade down Fifth Avenue in New York City.

Taking Blatch's cue, Alice Paul staged a parade for NAWSA in Washington, D.C., on March 3, 1913. The event, which featured floats and mounted brigades, attracted more than five thousand participants. It also drew angry mobs. When verbal violence became physical, troops had to intervene.

Paul's efforts were well planned. She had scheduled the NAWSA extravaganza for the day that the newly elected president, Woodrow Wilson, was due to arrive in the capital for his inauguration. While the inauguration normally would have prompted throngs of onlookers to greet the president, the highly anticipated crowds were attending the suffrage event instead. When one member of Wilson's staff finally asked, "Where are all the people?" a police officer informed him that they were at the parade. It did not take long for Wilson to recognize that this episode was a mere hint of the role the suffrage movement would play in his presidency. Wilson never demonstrated active support for the movement, however.

Thousands gather in Washington, D.C., on March 3, 1913, for the NAWSA parade.

"The whole art and practice of government consists not [of] moving individuals but [of] moving masses," Wilson declared to an audience of suffragists during the very same convention at which Catt delivered her "Crisis" address in September 1916. "It is all very well to run ahead and beckon, but, after all, you have got to wait for the body to follow. I have not come to ask you to be patient, because you have been, but I have come to congratulate you that there was a force behind you that will beyond any peradventure be triumphant and for which you can afford a little while to wait."

Though the president frequently spoke of NAWSA and its endeavors with admiration, he asked for patience regarding the passage of a constitutional amendment and expressed his opinion that the matter should be decided on a state-by-state basis. From the perspective of Catt and a number of other suffragists, it initially seemed prudent and productive to accept this approach and to work with—rather than against—it. Catt met with Wilson often, and while she argued for the need for immediate action on voting rights for women, she continued to support the president and his policies.

Paul, on the other hand, perceived no use in such methods and, like Stanton before her, opted to form a suffrage group separate and apart from NAWSA. Not long after Wilson's inauguration, she and Lucy Burns created the Congressional Union for Woman Suffrage, which evolved into the National Woman's Party (NWP) by 1916. The goal of the NWP was to unite women of all races, ethnicities, and socioeconomic backgrounds so that they could work together to improve the lot of female citizens in the United States. As of the second decade of the twentieth century, the primary ambition of the organization was to win the passage of the Nineteenth Amendment. Supporters of the NWP pushed for immediate suffrage on a nationwide scale, as opposed to gradual state-by-state approval.

Members of this group were more aggressive than NAWSA. They picketed the White House, staged hunger strikes, and engaged in acts of civil disobedience. In addition, Paul and her comrades encouraged the public to vote Republican, especially as Wilson—who had clearly failed to meet their expectations—was a Democrat. Few Americans, however, would consider abandoning the president, who had promised to keep the nation out of the war raging in Europe.

An NWP member pickets the White House in Washington, D.C.

War and a Widening Rift among Suffragists

World War I involved many European nations. The principal antagonists were Britain, France, and Russia on one side, and Germany and Austria on the other. On April 6, 1917, the United States entered the war on the British side. Wilson succeeded in generating anti-German feeling partly because 128 Americans died when a German submarine sank the British ocean liner *Lusitania* on May 7, 1915.

As U.S. troops were deployed and citizens adopted a renewed sense of patriotism, the suffrage movement—which had previously been gaining momentum and widespread public attention—temporarily took a backseat to international affairs. As one *New York Times* reader noted in a letter to the editor of that publication, "As it is true that 'no woman capable of deserving a vote at this hour has any time to waste on suffrage,' it is even truer regarding the men, whose every hour should be devoted to the tremendous task this [world] is facing."

Certain suffragists did not express completely disparate views. In keeping with their less-radical perspective, Catt and members of NAWSA voiced their support of Wilson and were concerned about the effect that Paul and the NWP forces would have on their cause. After all, it hardly seemed appropriate or conducive to gaining political support to picket the White House during a large-scale war.

Despite disapproval from NAWSA, however, Paul refused to back down. Members of the NWP continued to picket the White House (they had been doing so since January 1917), and in June 1917 they started carrying banners that directly challenged America's claim to be a liberated world power. Specifically, the signs mocked Wilson's wartime discussions with Russia that called upon that nation to join the United

Silent Sentinels

NWP picketers who stood vigil outside the White House in 1917 were referred to as "Silent Sentinels." Despite the bold words emblazoned on their banners, they remained quiet and determined; they disregarded the weather, warnings from police, and repeated jeers from passersby. From the perspective of these activists, the president's tactics were strikingly similar—at least in regard to his obvious silence. Wilson made few public comments about the demonstrations at the White House. As one of the sentinels noted, "He was utterly oblivious, apparently, of our presence here."

States in a bid to salvage democracies around the globe. "We, the women of America, tell you that America is not a democracy," read the banners. "Twenty million American women are denied the right to vote. President Wilson is the chief opponent of their moral enfranchisement. Help us make this nation really free. Tell our government it must liberate people before it can claim free Russia as an ally."

Public reaction was far from supportive. On June 20, hundreds of angry onlookers who objected to the suffragists' tactics attempted to tear down the banner. NWP leaders, however, remained as unwavering and outspoken as ever. They saw the war as an opportunity to remind U.S. citizens that not everyone in America enjoyed the right to a voice in government.

"We have ordered another banner with the same wording," retorted Paul, "and we intend to show it in the same place." Her words further inflamed those who took exception to the arguably militant practices of the NWP. NAWSA party members were quick to express their disapproval of Paul's intention.

The *New York Times* quoted Anna Shaw, the honorary president of the organization, as saying that "[such] agitation . . . was injurious to the suffrage cause." Catt voiced a similar perspective: "We [NAWSA] are not in any way in sympathy with the method that has been used by the White House pickets. . . . We consider it unwise, unpatriotic, and most unprofitable to the cause of suffrage." What disturbed NAWSA leaders was that the cause of suffrage had already faced tremendous opposition from a variety of factions long before Paul and the NWP had introduced their inflammatory tactics. The opposition's reasons ranged from arguments that had been put forth in the previous century to new assertions related to patriotism and social stability.

Three

Objections to the Movement

EVEN BEFORE THE UNITED STATES entered World War I, suf-fragists were arguing their cause in the face of wide-ranging opposition in the early twentieth century. For those Ameri-cans who believed it was best to keep women away from the polls, several age-old objections to the suffrage movement still carried weight well into the 1900s. Theodore Roosevelt, who was president from 1901 to 1909, reiterated several of these ideas in a letter drafted in 1908 to Lyman Abbott, a prominent theologian and author. Roosevelt wrote that granting women the vote threatened to disrupt the stability of a society that was rooted in preordained roles based on gender, such as female homemakers and caretakers and male decision makers and wage earners. Further, he pointed out that women did not seem to universally desire suffrage, a fact that made him feel less passionate about fighting to help them win it. Roosevelt proclaimed,

> Personally I believe in women's suffrage,
> but I am not an enthusiastic advocate
> of it because I do not regard it as a very
> important matter. I am unable to see that
> there has been any special improvement in

One early opponent of women's suffrage was Theodore Roosevelt.

the position of women in those states in the West that have adopted women's suffrage, as compared with those states adjoining them that have not adopted it. I do not think that giving the women suffrage will produce any marked improvement in the condition of women. I do not believe that it will produce any of the evils feared, and I am very certain that when women as a whole take any special interest in the matter they will have suffrage if they desire it.

But at present I think most of them are lukewarm; I find some actively for it and some actively against it. I am, for the reasons above given, rather what you would regard as lukewarm or tepid in my support of it because, while I believe in it, I do not regard it as of very much importance. I believe that man and woman should stand on an equality of right, but I do not believe that equality of right means identity of functions; and I am more and more convinced that the great field, the indispensable field, for the usefulness of woman is as the mother of the family.

It is her work in the household, in the home, her work in bearing and rearing the children, which is more important than any man's work, and it is the work which should be normally the woman's special work, just as normally the man's work should be that of the breadwinner, the supporter of the home, and, if necessary, the soldier who will fight for the home. There are exceptions as regards both man and woman; but the full and perfect life, the life of highest happiness and of highest usefulness to the state, is the life of the man and woman who are husband and wife, who live in the partnership of love and duty, the one earning enough to keep the home, the other managing the home and the children.

While some women disagreed with Roosevelt's assessment, others were quick to support it. Supporters, who in many cases formed their own antisuffrage organizations, believed that political matters were best left to male household heads and that any deviation from this philosophy would wreak havoc upon family life. From their perspective, there was no reason to support measures that would lay the weighty responsibilities of Washington upon the shoulders of ladies, who were best occupied by tending to responsibilities that more naturally fell to maternal caregivers, including child rearing and creating tranquil and productive homes. In 1917 the Nebraska Association Opposed to Woman Suffrage (NAOWS)—which was made up primarily of women—outlined such arguments in a pamphlet titled *Ten Reasons Why the Great Majority of Women Do Not Want the Ballot*. Members explained why women should not seek the vote:

> BECAUSE they have not lost faith in their
> fathers, husbands, sons, and brothers, who
> afford full protection to the community,
> there being no call for women to relieve
> them of the task. . . . BECAUSE in political
> activities there is constant strife, turmoil,
> contention, and bitterness, producing
> conditions from which every normal
> woman naturally shrinks. . . .
> BECAUSE woman suffrage will not
> enhance peace and harmony in the home,
> but, on the contrary, in the heat of a cam-
> paign, it is sure to bring about dissension
> and discord. . . .

Male and female antisuffragists also warned of social consequences that would result from a constitutional amendment giving women the right to vote. They predicted higher divorce rates, a larger and more disruptive presence of female laborers taking jobs outside the home, and the neglect of charities and other civic responsibilities to which ladies traditionally tended. In addition, several twentieth-century opponents of the movement predicted that many women — because they did not have the political sophistication to do otherwise — would simply vote as their husbands, brothers, and fathers did.

In fact, these arguments and opinions were not new; they dated back to the time of the first suffragists. World War I

One group that opposed women's voting rights was the National Association Opposed to Women's Suffrage. Here a group of men read materials at one of its stands in Washington, D.C., in 1910.

and the tension that Americans experienced subsequent to becoming involved in it set the stage for new and more heated objections to activists such as Paul and Burns, as well as to their perspectives and tactics.

Unpatriotic Picketers

Alice Paul's parade in 1913 had evoked curiosity and criticism yet had raised awareness of suffrage issues; the emotions that NWP pickets stirred in 1917 were harsher. "It is a shame," commented one observer, "that we have to give our sons to the service of the country and be confronted by such outrageous statements at the very White House gates." There were many Americans who might have been more sympathetic had the nation not been at war. To them, the picketing seemed scandalously unpatriotic.

With thousands of American soldiers fighting and dying for their country, discussing and debating what much of the public perceived as a trivial topic — a woman's right to vote — was a distraction from supporting the war effort. Many antisuffragists argued that it was not a good time to upturn America's entire social and political system by approving a constitutional amendment to give women the vote. Opponents of the movement — and even some of those men and women who had previously been undecided on the issue or were inclined to support female enfranchisement — rejected the tactics of the NWP in the midst of the war. To stand by as members of Paul's organization openly criticized President Wilson and his definition of democracy seemed to border on a lack of patriotism.

"Why don't you take that banner to Berlin?" and angry shouts of "outrage" and "treason" frequently filled the air as picketers stood in determined silence outside the White House in June 1917. Police warned suffragists that their continued protests would likely result in imprisonment, but equally dramatic was the reaction of several key political figures who had previously endorsed women's voting rights. Several U.S. congressmen expressed their distaste for the banners that Paul and her fellow activists proudly held in their attempt to keep the public's attention on the suffrage movement.

"As one who believes in the principle of [women's] suffrage, I can only say that such an incident makes it exceedingly difficult to . . . continue to support the cause," admitted U.S. Representative Simeon Davison Fess. "There is no justification whatever for the flaunting of such a banner." Police in Washington, D.C., agreed, and arrests began when similar demonstrations were organized in the months ahead, usually under charges of obstructing traffic.

President Wilson offered little public comment on the picketers or their impact on American suffrage. By that point, he had earned a reputation for praising the work of more conservative suffragists, such as Catt, but he was clearly not inclined to act with any particular haste in furthering their efforts. Nor did the president's administration appear to object when law enforcement officials began to handcuff members of the NWP and send them to prison. Burns, Paul, and other activists eventually served time in jail, where they maintained an aggressive protest against Wilson's lack of advocacy of a constitutional amendment. Ironically, it was their incarceration that ultimately played a major role in reshaping the opinions of many Americans who had previously opposed their demonstrations and had objected to their fight for the vote.

What Have We Come to in America?

From the perspective of suffragists who were jailed for picketing the White House in 1917, their imprisonment was reflective of a nation that was in dire need of reform. In disregard of the unpopularity of expressing such views during wartime, most activists did not hesitate to voice their sentiments. "What have we come to in America," asked the NWP member and benefactress Alva Belmont, "when splendid women, loving liberty, are arrested for asking this simple question: 'Mr. President, in your message to Congress, urge the passage of the federal suffrage amendment enfranchising women'?" Though not all Americans initially shared Belmont's opinion, an increasing number changed their minds after suffragists proved their valor from behind bars.

Perspectives after Occoquan Workhouse

Life behind bars was designed to be more than a mere slap on the hand for imprisoned suffragists. Officials hoped to force Paul, Burns, and other members of the NWP who were being housed at Occoquan Workhouse, in Occoquan, Virginia, into submission. Yet the incarcerated activists were not willing to readily abandon their mission. In fact, they went so far as to lead hunger strikes in a display of civil disobedience. In turn, Paul, Burns, and their companions were often force-fed by prison officials; tubes were shoved up their noses to prevent suffocation and, ostensibly, their martyrdom. The suffragists also endured harassment from wardens that ranged from physical brutality to having their hands handcuffed above their heads in their cells. Many of these women, who numbered approximately 168 by 1920, were primarily from the middle and upper classes and had no previous experience as political prisoners.

"We were thrust into cells; the ventilators were closed," recounted the NWP activist Paula Jakobi of her incarceration in November 1917. "The cells were bitter cold. There was an open toilet in the corner of the cell, which was flushed from the outside. We had to call a guard who had previously attacked us to flush [it]. The doors were barred, there were no windows. . . . There was no light in the room, only one in the corridor. . . . The floors were filthy, as were the blankets."

Jakobi and her fellow prisoners were denied communication with the outside world, as news of the activists' tribulations undoubtedly would have garnered sympathy for them and enthusiasm for their cause, as well as disapproval

A suffrage poster intended to raise public awareness about the abuse of imprisoned activists.

of the prison and government systems that allowed American women to be treated in such a fashion. Ultimately, however, word of their trials did pass beyond the walls of Occoquan, and the same members of the public and Washington, D.C.'s, political scene that had formerly condemned the NWP's tactics suddenly rose to that organization's defense.

Neither President Wilson nor anyone else in the capital wanted to be linked to something that might reasonably be called torture. Further, much of the general public was both shocked at what the activists were enduring at the hands of the government and impressed by their unwavering devotion to their movement. Americans across the country redirected their outrage from the White House picketers to Wilson and others who allowed the political imprisonment to continue. A cry rose up to release the ladies who represented the NWP and, on a larger scale, a courageous and unyielding battle to win constitutional change.

"It is time that the sportsmanship and gallantry of American men and . . . the humanity and political power of the women voters of the state of New York and of the Western states spoke out against this conduct of the government," declared Dudley Field Malone, who served as legal counsel for Paul, in November 1917. Dr. John Winters Brannan, the husband of another suffragist imprisoned at Occoquan, expressed similar sentiments and added that—regardless of whether or not an individual was in favor of giving women the vote—it was impossible not to admire the spirit and suffering that defined the activists' efforts. "These facts represent an intolerable condition that cannot be permitted to go on," noted Brannan of the situation at the workhouse. "Whether we agree with these ladies or not in the methods they employ to win a share in our government, we are compelled to recognize their sincerity and sacrifice."

Burns, Paul, and the other suffragists were released from Occoquan during the last week of November 1917 after spending about half a year in incarceration; by the time of their release, the movement had gained a much needed boost of public sympathy, support, and awareness. It was by now obvious to President Wilson, as well as to average citizens, that the suffragists were deeply committed to their cause. The lengths to which they were willing to go to jeopardize their physical and emotional comfort and safety captured America's attention. Wilson and others, more or less reluctantly, conceded that women deserved the voting rights that the Nineteenth Amendment embodied.

Four

Political Viewpoints on the Nineteenth Amendment

THOUGH WORLD WAR I HAD INITIALLY seemed to detract attention from the suffragists and had even aroused disdain from citizens who believed their efforts were unpatriotic, few former critics could deny the significant role women played during the international crisis. The tens of thousands of U.S. troops deployed to fight overseas left an appreciable void in several areas of life on the home front. Just as they had done in so many prior conflicts that involved the United States, women rose to the challenge and dedicated their efforts to preserving stability while their husbands, fathers, and brothers were away. They did everything: assembled weapons, stitched uniforms and flags, served as medical personnel and took on the duties of head of household in the absence of their husbands and fathers.

As mentioned above, President Wilson found it ever harder to oppose suffrage by early 1918. In addition to the positive publicity the NWP—and the suffrage movement in general—had garnered after the events at Occoquan Workhouse had been revealed, it was difficult to argue that women did not deserve a voice in national affairs when they were making undeniable contributions to the war effort.

As American men left the country to fight in World War I, their wives, mothers, and sisters entered the workforce in greater numbers.

Wilson realized that it was no longer practical or even politically prudent for him to urge patience and state-by-state ratification of women's voting rights.

After all, it was not merely female citizens in select regions who had answered the call to duty during World War I—women across the nation had responded to the country's needs as the fighting continued. Further, thanks to the strategies of the NWP, the issue of suffrage had become politically divisive on party lines. When Paul and Burns urged voters to boycott Democratic candidates, they gave the Republicans a potential head start in the presidential election of 1920. If Wilson failed to take a public stand in favor of a constitutional amendment that would guarantee women's suffrage, he was essentially casting undecided voters in the direction of a candidate from the opposition party.

These factors, coupled with the suffragists' clear message that they would not be ignored, prompted the president to finally announce his advocacy of the Nineteenth Amendment on January 9, 1918. That day, a committee of Democrats at long last reported that "the president had not felt at liberty to volunteer his advice to members of Congress on this important matter, but, when his advice was sought, he very frankly and earnestly advised us to vote for the amendment, as an act of right and justice to the women of the country and of the world."

Though adoption of the amendment still depended on subsequent votes in both houses of Congress and in state legislatures, the sensation of having won a substantial victory rippled through suffrage camps of all persuasions, from the radical NWP to the more conservatively inclined NAWSA. Once Wilson altered his public perspective on granting women the vote, female activists appeared to express a more positive opinion of the president, as well.

On January 9, 1918, President Woodrow Wilson finally voiced his complete support of the Nineteenth Amendment.

Suffragists also seemed to share a universal—if somewhat guarded—sense of optimism that triumph was imminent.

"It is difficult to express our gratification at the president's stand," reflected Paul. "For four years, we have striven to secure his support for the national amendment, for we knew that it—and perhaps it alone—would ensure our success. It means to us only one thing—victory. Six-sevenths of the Republicans have already pledged their votes. The Democrats will undoubtedly follow their great leader. It is only the women who have labored and sacrificed who know fully what victory means, but all Americans must be proud to have our country join the liberal nations of the world in which women share full liberty with men."

Speaking on behalf of NAWSA, Shaw echoed Paul's sentiments with the simple, "Onward with our president, the great leader of democracy!" Even in light of Wilson's stance, the Nineteenth Amendment was far from ready to be written into America's law books. Two-thirds of the Senate and the House of Representatives had to ratify the proposed addition to the Constitution, and 75 percent of the states subsequently had to do the same. Put more simply, the majority of politicians both on a national and statewide basis had to accept and agree with the idea that, in the language of the proposed amendment, "the right of citizens of the United States to vote shall not be denied or abridged by the United States or by any state on account of sex." Despite the president's change of heart, not every man who possessed political power was ready to reform his opinions on the topic of women's suffrage.

Women's Rights or States' Rights?
On January 10, 1918—just a day after Wilson handed down his declaration of support—members of the U.S. House of Representatives voted in favor of women's suffrage. Exactly 274 representatives, about two-thirds of the House members, voted yea. It was a year and a half later before the Senate acted similarly.

Despite the House's stance, several of the senators continued to push for a gradual state-by-state acceptance of suffrage rather than a comprehensive amendment. Certain congressmen saw the rights of women, though worthy of discussion and debate, as a matter to be decided by individual state legislatures. All politicians were keenly aware that, regardless of their personal opinions, voting in a manner that was displeasing to the citizens they represented could very likely cost them reelection. More often than not, however, they publicly proclaimed that their perspectives were related to respecting the wishes of state government, versus admitting any connection to their own careers and advancement. Senator James W. Wadsworth Jr. of New York rationalized,

> No vote of mine cast upon this amendment
> would deprive any of the electors of my
> state of any privilege they now enjoy. I feel
> so strongly that the people of the several
> states should be permitted to decide for
> themselves that [I] am frank to say that, if
> this amendment, instead of being drafted to
> extend woman suffrage all over the country,
> were drafted to forbid the extension of the
> franchise to women in the states, I would
> vote against it. Even though one might
> be opposed on general principles to the
> extension of the franchise to women, one
> cannot logically object to the people of a
> state settling that question for themselves.
> It seems to me that it is incumbent upon a
> senator in considering his attitude on this
> matter to regard the nation as a whole and to

give consideration to the wishes of the people
of the various states [that] have expressed
themselves from time to time.

In September 1918 President Wilson challenged Wadsworth's views and those of other nonsupporters of the Nineteenth Amendment during his address to the Senate.

"We have made partners of the women in this war," Wilson observed. "Shall we admit them only to a partnership of suffering and sacrifice and toil and not to a partnership of privilege and right?" Despite the president's urging, the Senate failed to pass the proposed amendment by the required two-thirds vote. Yet politicians' opinions did appear to be changing, as that autumn's senatorial tally fell short of the necessary majority by only two ballots. As the months passed, the suffragists did not rest from lobbying for their cause, and their endeavors finally reached fruition in June 1919, when sixty-six senators (two more than needed) endorsed the Nineteenth Amendment.

Proponents of women's voting rights were ecstatic to be so close at last to obtaining the constitutional change that had first been proposed by founders of the suffrage movement in the previous century. The taste of victory they savored in June 1919 was just that, a sampling of success— and a simultaneous reminder of the battle that still lay ahead. The amendment process required 75 percent of the forty-eight states to ratify the proposed amendment. Thus, ratification by thirty-six states was needed. Only then would the amendment become part of the Constitution. Though the suffragists realized that they still had much work to do, most were buoyed by the Senate's recent stance.

An Issue of No Great Urgency

For James Wadsworth and other like-minded congressmen, female suffrage was not an issue that warranted a constitutional amendment. Wadsworth considered it a matter best left to the states, "Now the question is whether the people of these states are competent to settle the question for themselves. There is no tremendous emergency facing the country, no revolution or rebellion threatened, which would seem to make it necessary to impose on the people of these states a thing they have said as free citizens they do not require or desire. Is it contrary to the spirit of American institutions that they shall be left free to decide these things for themselves?"

"The last stage of the fight is to obtain ratification of the amendment, so women may vote in the presidential election in 1920," remarked Catt. "This we are confident will be achieved. The friends of woman suffrage in both parties have carried out their word. In the result, we can turn our backs upon the end of a long and arduous struggle, needlessly darkened and embittered by the stubbornness of a few at the expense of the many. 'Eyes front' is the watchword as we turn upon the struggle for ratification by the states."

Red versus Yellow

As suffragists began to map out their plan for winning individual states, they were confident that they had the support of at least Wyoming, Colorado, Utah, Idaho, Washington, California, Kansas, Arizona, Oregon, Montana, New York, Oklahoma, South Dakota, Michigan, Illinois, Nebraska, Rhode Island, North Dakota, Iowa, Wisconsin, Indiana, Maine, Minnesota, Missouri, Tennessee, Arkansas, Nevada, and Texas—states that already had granted women complete or at least presidential suffrage.

Unlikely to bend in favor of the Nineteenth Amendment were legislatures from southern states and New England. Lawmakers from the South had been largely opposed to voting rights for African Americans in the late 1800s, and they were similarly opposed to extending that privilege to female citizens. To conservative senators and representatives from the Northeast, the enfranchisement of women was considered rather a radical issue.

Many of the political leaders in western states had previously voiced their support of the amendment or ratified it, and so the suffragists continued their protests, speeches, and picket lines in regions that were still undecided and potentially persuadable on the issue. By March 1920, thirty-five of thirty-six states had said yes to the Nineteenth Amendment, and activists pushed more aggressively than ever to recruit one final state to their cause.

As the summer of 1920 progressed, Tennessee legislators appeared to be the most likely to give supporters of suffrage the tally they needed to win. A victory in Nashville, Tennessee, however, was by no means an assumption that lobbyists could take for granted. So, in August of that year, Catt and other suffrage leaders, as well as reporters, descended upon the city for one last push to promote the amendment. Thus, Nashville became the site of what was later referred to as the War of the Roses—a conflict between proponents of suffrage, who famously wore yellow roses to symbolize their political perspectives, and antisuffragists, who opted for red roses on their lapels.

The state senate approved the amendment on August 18, 1920, but it was clear that the vote in the state's house of representatives would be close. After a day full of speeches that reflected sentiments both for and against women's voting rights, House Speaker Seth Walker, who was renowned for his antisuffrage views, proclaimed, "The hour has come. The battle has been fought and won, and I move . . . that the motion to concur in the Senate action goes where it belongs—to the table."

By advising that the issue be tabled—that is, that further discussion be postponed until the next legislative session in late fall—Walker might have temporarily cost the suffragists their much-needed victory. Luckily for those in favor of the amendment, members of the House could not form a majority.

A Never-Ending Push to Maintain Public Awareness

When Connecticut and Vermont governors refused to call special sessions to ratify the Nineteenth Amendment, members of the NWP marched in protest. Just as the battle over the constitutional change seemed to reach a climax, the suffragists' efforts to capture and maintain public awareness appeared more challenged than ever.

"The women . . . carried their purple, white and gold banner, which sought, in a variety of slogans, to place responsibility for failure to ratify the amendment squarely upon the Republican Party and to set forth all the bad things 17,000,000 women could and would do to that party next November if it did not get busy right away and make national enfranchisement an accomplished fact," read a *New York Times* article that chronicled the NWP picket against the north-eastern governors in June 1920. "Silently the women moved along the curb . . . but . . . a vast majority of the hurrying thousands did not even notice them." From the perspective of much of the American public, the biggest hurdle the suffragists had to surmount had been overcome when President Wilson and Congress offered their backing. Though the issue of women's voting rights was still on the minds of average Americans, not all of them appreciated the tremendous pressure that activists faced when the passage of the Nineteenth Amendment was finally so close to becoming a reality.

Votes both for and against tabling the amendment came in deadlocked at forty-eight to forty-eight. A second vote resulted in the same counts. Legislators finally agreed to debate the suffrage amendment during the current session, and the amendment was soon put to a vote.

To the shock of onlookers, as well as his fellow congressmen, twenty-four-year-old Harry T. Burn, who had previously sported a red rose, handed down an "aye" vote to break the tie. The surprised supporters of the amendment wept with gratitude and cheered with delight, while antisuffragists made such a din that the young politician was forced to retreat to the capitol attic. Whether those around him were exhilarated or outraged, however, few could have guessed what had prompted Burn to alter his perspective within such a short time. When Burn explained the reasoning behind his change of heart, they discovered that the source of his shift was, quite appropriately, a woman. "I know that a mother's advice is always safest for a boy to follow," Burn said, adding that he had recently received a note with the following instructions from his own mother: "Hurrah and vote for suffrage. Don't keep them in doubt. . . . I have been watching how you stood but have not seen anything yet. Don't forget to be a good boy and help Mrs. Catt."

Burn's vote prompted another representative to speak out in favor of suffrage, as well. The new tally of fifty representatives in favor of the amendment and forty-six against promised victory to its supporters. On August 24, 1920, Governor A. H. Roberts signed a resolution that officially reflected his state's ratification of suffrage, and two days later, the Nineteenth

Alice Paul unfurls a banner in Washington, D.C., on August 13, 1920, in celebration of Tennessee's ratification of the Nineteenth Amendment.

Amendment, also referred to as the Susan B. Anthony Amendment, was added to the U.S. Constitution.

Though the passage of the amendment guaranteed women the right to vote, in the years that followed, not all women were able to exercise this right—and not all Americans supported their desire to do so.

Five

Voting Rights and Realities after 1920

THE PRESIDENTIAL ELECTION OF 1920 marked the first major political race in which American women across the nation were guaranteed the constitutional right to play a role at the polls. Yet, just as opinions had varied on the idea of ladies heading to the ballot box before the passage of the Nineteenth Amendment, so were they diverse mere months after the suffragists' victory in Tennessee. In the election, in which the Republican candidate Warren G. Harding won against the Democrat James M. Cox, the *New York Times* approximated that only one in every three women in New York State voted, as opposed to an estimated two out of three men. In certain states, such as Mississippi and Georgia, the timing of the passage of the amendment and the requirement that all voters register at least four months prior to an election created problems for female citizens who might otherwise have cast a ballot. Catt was nonetheless of the opinion that the presence of women at the polls that year was testimony to the merit of the Nineteenth Amendment.

"The presidential election was the first test of universal suffrage in the United States," she observed. "It is estimated that between 28 million and 30 million votes were cast, as

compared with 18 million in 1916. This is the largest vote
ever cast in any country." As an explanation for the dispari-
ties between the number of men and women who cast ballots,
Catt added the following:

> The vote came to women in many states
> too late for the best preparatory work to
> be done. Political parties tried to get their
> own women to register and vote the straight
> ticket. . . . Had the vote [for the Nineteenth
> Amendment] come earlier, more women
> would have voted, and more women would
> have trained for election work. On the
> whole, women liked the vote, and men
> liked to have them vote. The timid who
> ventured into politics with many reservations
> found the casting of a vote easier and more
> interesting than they had supposed. . . .
> Women have good and sufficient reason to
> be fairly well satisfied with this, their first
> participation in a great national contest.

Catt's NAWSA colleague Nettie R. Shuler took a somewhat harsher perspective of ladies who did not stand in line
at the polls in November 1920. "No groups of women I know
refrained from voting," she noted.

> The only groups that seemed uninterested
> were the women who belong to the bridge-
> playing classes — the parasitic women who do
> nothing but amuse themselves. I do not think

Women stand in line with men in New York City on November 2, 1920, to cast their votes in that year's presidential election.

that they, as a whole, did not vote. They, however, were not willing to take much trouble. They are not the ultra-smart women, nor are they anti-suffragists. These did vote and were interested in the election. It was chiefly the light, amusement-seeking type who did not respond.

Regardless of Catt's and Shuler's varying justifications for why more women did not participate, it was the overall increased volume of female voters in 1920 that was most headline worthy — not the mere presence of the ladies themselves. After all, women had been allowed to vote in presidential elections in certain states since the 1800s. Thus, men and antisuffragists were, by and large, not openly hostile or scandalized simply because a voter with a corset could suddenly cast a ballot.

One male editorialist summed up his perspective on what he hoped would come of the Nineteenth Amendment in the *New York Times* on November 6, 1920. "The women voters, newly come into the possession of the privilege they so long have sought, have a duty they cannot evade without discredit. They must show the country that the privilege they will exercise was not unworthily conferred. As new voters, they are not obliged to be unthinking partisans, to vote just as their fathers, husbands, [and] brothers vote. They are under a higher moral obligation to vote intelligently." As the editorialist — and the rest of the world — would learn in the years ahead, female voters would not fail in fulfilling this expectation, but many would face some significant obstacles in being able to take advantage of the constitutional right they had been guaranteed in 1920.

Civil Rights and Voting Rights

While the presence of women at the polls began to have significant political impact starting in the 1950s, several female citizens were still unable to cast a ballot. For example, per the Fifteenth and Nineteenth amendments, African-American women technically had the constitutional right to vote. However, state governments — especially in the South — often had various registration restrictions in place, including residency

Alice Paul's Second Proposed Amendment

What became of the fiery NWP leader Alice Paul following the ratification of the Nineteenth Amendment? During the 1920s she dedicated her efforts to the passage of yet another constitutional change—the Equal Rights Amendment (ERA). When she introduced the amendment at the seventy-fifth anniversary of the Seneca Falls Convention in 1923, she proposed that it include the following: "Men and women shall have equal rights throughout the United States and every place subject to its jurisdiction." Essentially, Paul hoped to eradicate any form of discrimination on the basis of gender and to guarantee that all the privileges inherent to the U.S. Constitution—not merely suffrage— would be granted to women.

The text of Paul's proposed amendment has been modified several times over the years and currently reads, "Equality of rights under the law shall not be denied or abridged by the United States or any state on account of sex." While state governments and the U.S. Congress have considered and debated the ERA, it still has not received enough timely support to be added to the U.S. Constitution. The amendment's opponents have noted that it has far-reaching implications that could drastically impact legislation related to topics such as labor and abortion rights. Advocates of the ERA continue to fight for its passage.

requirements and literacy tests. The poll tax (a fee that a citizen had to pay in order to vote) was yet another hindrance.

Such measures, coupled in certain instances with racial intimidation, prompted some African Americans, Hispanics, and American Indians, both men and women, to stay away from voting booths. These individuals, along with poor whites in primarily rural areas, were not always literate or might be unable to afford a poll tax. When a poor family was able to scrape enough together to pay for one member to register to vote, that member was often the male head of the household. In addition, there were still some minority women who feared for their physical safety at the hands of the Ku Klux Klan or similar groups should they go to the polls. Klan members—who by the 1950s were far less numerous than they had been two decades earlier—sometimes employed arson, vandalism, personal violence, and occasionally even murder to keep black people from voting.

Fannie Lou Hamer, an African-American civil rights activist, was unjustly imprisoned in Winona, Mississippi, in 1963 after attending a voter-registration workshop. Local police beat her so badly that she lost sensation in her legs. Soon after, Hamer became one of the founders of the Mississippi Freedom Democratic Party (MFDP), a political group organized to challenge the established Democratic Party. She and other MFDP members argued that regular Democrats were mostly politicians who had been elected only because African Americans had been deprived of their voting rights.

"If the Freedom Democratic Party isn't seated today, I question America," Hamer proclaimed at the 1964 Democratic National Convention, in Atlantic City. "Is this America where we have to sleep with our phones off the hooks because we be threatened daily just 'cause we want to register to vote to become first class citizens?" Other activists of both genders and all races combatted restrictive registration practices by forming community organizations to promote voter education and awareness. They also called for an end to discriminatory measures implemented by state governments.

Fannie Lou Hamer enters the Democratic National Convention Hall in Atlantic City, New Jersey, in 1964, after she and other African Americans were previously denied entry.

Their efforts sometimes produced a backlash, even harassment and violence, from certain white people, especially in the Deep South, who neither wanted nor saw the need for change at the ballot box. Americans who supported poll taxes and literacy requirements believed that such measures helped ensure that only intelligent, qualified voters had a say in political affairs. Activists, however, considered this argument usually a convenient rationalization to disguise racial or sex-based hostility.

"Voting is not a 'right,' in the sense that a person is born entitled to it," noted members of an Alabama commission who opposed unrestricted suffrage during the 1960s. "Else we would register the babies to vote!" Voting-rights advocates interpreted this statement to mean that women and non-Caucasians were not necessarily entitled to cast a ballot, despite constitutional guarantees. Unconvinced by the Nineteenth Amendment, some Americans still maintained that females had little more place than children at polling booths.

The onset of the civil rights movement in the 1960s saw voter-registration campaigns become increasingly effective and widespread. Protestors, public speakers, politicians, and average citizens pushed for equal access to the voting booth; activists demanded that race and sex be eliminated from the context of voting rights. Their endeavors bore fruit with the ratification of the Twenty-fourth Amendment (1964), which eliminated poll taxes in federal elections. The following year, the Voting Rights Act was signed into law; it effectively banned literacy tests, authorized the federal government to handle voter registration in portions of the country that had a reputation for discriminating against its minority citizens, and even permitted voters not fluent in English to cast a ballot. Addressing Congress prior to the act's passage, President Lyndon B. Johnson expressed his support of the legislation.

> To those who seek to avoid action by their national government in their home communities . . . who seek to maintain purely local control over elections—the answer is simple. Open your polling places to all your people. Allow men and women to register and vote, whatever the color of their skin. Extend the rights of citizenship to every citizen of this land. There is no constitutional issue here. The command of the Constitution is plain. There is no moral issue. It is wrong—deadly wrong—to deny any of your fellow-Americans the right to vote in this country. There is no issue of states rights or national rights. There is only the struggle for human rights.

Global Suffrage in the Twenty-first Century

By the late 1960s, it appeared that the changes suffragists had sought for decades prior to 1920 were truly transforming voting rights into a reality for women across the country. Nevertheless, nearly a century after Catt, Paul, and other suffragists had succeeded in legally enfranchising American women, not every other nation's women had won the same right.

"Unfortunately, there are still countries that do not recognize the valuable resource that women provide," declared Kris Myers, the director of Heritage and Outreach at the Alice Paul Institute (API) of Mount Laurel, New Jersey, during a 2008 interview.

> There are those who simply do not believe
> that women are the same type of human
> beings as men are, with the same abilities
> to think and contribute to society. Some
> [nations] simply do not think about women.
> On agendas that include politics and
> economy, they do not consider women.
> Until they do, they close one-half of their
> entire population out of the opportunity to
> contribute to their own country. How can
> a country represent their people on a world
> stage if they represent only one-half—or
> less—of their people?

Lebanon, Brunei, Saudi Arabia, the United Arab Emirates, and Vatican City are currently the five locations across the globe that, as of 2010, continue to deny complete voting rights to females. Despite Myers's observations, there are myriad reasons why such nations do not extend suffrage to women. For example, Brunei is a sultanate; none of its citizens can vote. The United Arab Emirates, however, has been restructuring its voting process with the goal of granting suffrage to both men and women by 2010.

Certain countries allow female citizens to vote but restrict their ability to do so. In Lebanon, women must demonstrate

Questioning the Significance of Suffrage in Saudi Arabia

Some women in Saudi Arabia are anxious to achieve suffrage but by no means all. Among the latter group are those who feel that, given their limited interactions with men in a largely male-dominated culture, their vote would have little significance.

"We aren't [equal]," noted Sarah Muhammad of Saudi Arabia in 2004. "We have so little interaction with men that we will vote with our emotions, choosing candidates for their looks and sweet talk rather than for what they can deliver." Saudi resident Rima Khaled expressed similar sentiments with regard to the issue of suffrage. "What's the point of voting?" she questioned. "Even if we did vote, we would go home to the men in our lives who will have the last say in whatever we do."

proof of an elementary education to cast a ballot, though men need not do so. As for Vatican City, elections occur only during papal conclaves, when the world's cardinals gather to elect a new pope. The Roman Catholic Church does not permit women to become cardinals. In Saudi Arabia, elections have only recently been restored. Women, however, are excluded from the process.

Many female citizens of these nations regard the aforementioned reasons for their lack of suffrage as far from adequate. "Women are capable of voting and making the right choices," said Nour Ahmed, a marketing graduate from Saudi Arabia, during a 2004 interview. "Why aren't men and women equal in this issue?" According to a Saudi businesswoman, Rasha Hifzi, Ahmed's argument needs to be explained to more than her country's male population. American suffragists realized in the late 1800s and early 1900s that part of the struggle was convincing women to stand up and fight for their rights; their present-day Saudi counterparts are grappling with the same realization.

"We're working to lobby for women to participate in the elections," said Hifzi in 2008. "But the most important thing, if we want the government to help us in letting women participate in the elections, [is that] we need to have the demand from the civic society and from the women themselves because if they are careless and they don't believe in elections, nobody will vote, [and] we'll have no candidates." Others among the few spots around the globe that do not presently extend full voting rights to women seem to be making strides toward widening the electoral process.

In addition, certain international organizations, particularly the United Nations, are working to make universal

Women in Saudi Arabia are not permitted to vote in national elections.

suffrage a worldwide phenomenon. The fact that there are still women elsewhere in the world whose ability to express their political opinions is incomplete should suffice to give their American female counterparts pause. It has been argued that the absence of universal enfranchisement ought to lead U.S. citizens to consider whether voting is a privilege or an obligation. At the least, today's Americans might profit from reflecting upon the events of 1920 and their subsequent effect upon the United States.

Six

Modern Perspectives on the Amendment

THE PRESIDENTIAL ELECTION OF 2008 occurred eighty-eight years after American suffragists won their cause. As twenty-first-century voters cast their ballots, it was obvious that the role of gender in national politics had changed greatly since Paul, Catt, and their counterparts rallied for enfranchisement. Hillary Clinton and Sarah Palin were the most prominent of many female politicians who played significant parts in the 2008 White House race. Palin succeeded in becoming the Republican vice presidential nominee.

It could hardly be contested that female citizens had secured a decisive voice in national affairs, whether in or out of government. The voter turnout in the 2008 national election reached 64.1 percent—the highest since 1908. State and local races generally had lower turnouts, but whatever the actual cause—disenchantment with candidates, disgust or apathy toward politics, or any one of several others—it could no longer be argued that women had been denied a voice. How an American, male or female, views voting—as a right or a responsibility—has ceased to be a matter that someone else has the power to decide. It is worth keeping in mind, however, that many people, now long dead, struggled long and hard to place today's Americans in an enviable position.

More than eighty years after the passing of the Nineteenth Amendment, Hillary Clinton (left) and Sarah Palin (right) took part in the race for the White House in 2008.

"Normally, I would look at voting merely as a right," declared Laura Piché, a graduate student from Denver, Colorado, when interviewed in 2009. "But it's hard not to view it as a duty, as well, when you consider that people were leading hunger strikes in prison cells just so women like me would one day be able to take part in the country's political process. I think that knowing what the suffragists did kind of motivates me to become more involved in or at least knowledgeable about politics in general." Another registered voter, Pat Spilseth, of Wayzata, Minnesota, expressed similar sentiments during a 2008 interview. "I consider voting to be the right *and* the obligation of every citizen of the United States of America," Spilseth, who is a writer,

The Suffragists' Story Lives on

Founded in 1984, the Alice Paul Institute (API) in Mount Laurel, New Jersey, has restored Paul's birthplace and home, maintains a collection of her writings and personal memorabilia, and hosts leadership programs for eighth-grade girls. As the institute's Kris Myers explained, the aim is to make modern generations better aware of the women who played pivotal roles in the events leading up to universal suffrage. "The heroes Americans celebrate are courageous, shrewd, determined, and passionate about [their country]. The suffragists display all of these qualities and more. They wanted to participate in a democracy so much that they launched a seventy-two-year campaign for the right to vote. The ideas and tactics that emerged from the movement were creative and original. This is an important history to teach younger generations and an important contribution to the American story."

emphasized. "Perhaps there would be more voters if our classrooms educated us in meaningful manners that touched our hearts and minds [in regard to] what suffering has occurred with people who have fought for voting rights."

Despite such testimonials, it is far from clear how much interest modern men and women have in the history of the suffrage movement. Few voters recognize names such as Carrie Chapman Catt and Alice Paul, and fewer still understand their significance.

Twenty-First-Century Takes on the Events of 1920

As with all major events, the ratification of the Nineteenth Amendment runs the inevitable risk of becoming no more than an episode in history's ongoing saga. Yesterday's hunger strikes, political debates, losses, and victories can easily be overshadowed by the issues and dilemmas of today. Kris Myers believes that many U.S. citizens are not fully aware of the circumstances leading up to the triumph of 1920.

"Unfortunately," she noted, "when people hear the phrase 'women's history,' they assume it only pertains to women. The same happens with the Nineteenth Amendment, and you don't necessarily see it discussed in historical text because the topic is considered specialized. But many women and men have contacted me to say how proud they felt of the suffragists when they heard about how they went to jail for the vote. Most say, 'I never knew this happened here in America.' They are shocked, not only because of the lengths women went through for the vote, but because they never had the chance to learn about this incredible story." Melissa Kennedy, a librarian from River Forest, Illinois, also communicated (2008) her belief that the suffrage movement's history could be an inspiration to twenty-first-century citizens. She hastened to add, however, that the passage of time and other factors affect modern perspectives.

"I would hope more people would vote [if they were aware of what the suffragists went through]," observed Kennedy, "but I kind of doubt it. It seems so long ago and possibly has been a bit overshadowed by the civil rights movement." With seemingly few guarantees that present-day Americans will understand and appreciate the significance of the Nineteenth Amendment, growing public indifference toward and distaste for the political process is not out of the question.

"The younger generation is often blamed for being apathetic about political matters — particularly voting," Myers explained. "But the history of the lengths [to which] women went for the vote is one that young men and women won't [frequently] find in their history textbooks. So how can they understand why the vote is important when they don't know what it took to give them that right? I have seen young men and women become passionate about issues — when they learn about them and when they are invited to get involved. I believe that, with an opportunity to learn these issues, younger generations will . . . respond in overwhelming numbers."

Commemorating a Historic Constitutional Change

The federal government and women's groups work to convince modern-day citizens of the significance of the suffrage movement. In 1971, Congress declared August 26 Women's Equality Day to commemorate the passage of the Nineteenth Amendment and to persuade women that retaining equal rights is an ongoing battle. Politicians and motivational speakers often use this date as an occasion to celebrate how far the country has come and declare how far it still could go. They frequently remind listeners of the dedicated women of a century and more ago, who labored to overcome an environment where women's suffrage was largely a jest that amused everyone from national leaders to husbands, brothers, and fathers perusing the evening paper.

Other vehicles for keeping Americans' interest in the Nineteenth Amendment alive are museums, books, artwork, and films. Some of these means, though decades old, remain resonant in the twenty-first century. They reveal the frustration and dedication of the women who fought a hard fight to expand constitutional rights. The poem "Women," by the suffragist Alice Duer Miller, though published in 1915, expresses its aims and attitudes in plain and even somewhat crude terms.

> I went to ask my government if they would set
> me free,
> They gave a pardoned crook a vote, but hadn't
> one for me;
> The men about me laughed and frowned and
> said: 'Go home, because
> We really can't be bothered when we're busy
> making laws.'
> Oh, it's women this, and women that and
> women have no sense,
> But it's pay your taxes promptly when it comes
> to the expense,
> It comes to the — — expense, my dears, it
> comes to the — — expense,

In Commemoration of That Day . . .

A joint resolution of Congress in 1971 proclaimed Women's Equality Day with the following resolution:

> *Whereas, the women of the United States have been treated as second-class citizens and have not been entitled the full rights and privileges, public or private, legal or institutional, which are available to male citizens of the United States; and whereas, the women of the United States have united to assure that these rights and privileges are available to all citizens equally regardless of sex; and whereas, the women of the United States have designated August 26, the anniversary date of the passage of the Nineteenth*

Amendment, as symbol of the continued fight for equal rights: and, whereas the women of United States are to be commended and supported in their organizations and activities, now, therefore, be it resolved, the Senate and House of Representatives of the United States of America in Congress assembled, that August 26th of each year is designated as Women's Equality Day, and the president is authorized and requested to issue a proclamation annually in commemoration of that day in 1920, on which the women of America were first given the right to vote, and that day in 1970, on which a nationwide demonstration for women's rights took place.

It's pay your — — taxes promptly when it
　　comes to the — — expense.
I went into a factory to earn my daily bread:
Men said: 'The home is woman's sphere.' 'I
　　have no home,' I said.
But when the men all marched to war, they
　　cried to wife and maid,
'Oh, never mind about the home, but save the
　　export trade.'
For it's women this and women that, and
　　home's the place for you,
But it's patriotic angels when there's outside
　　work to do,
There's outside work to do, my dears, there's
　　outside work to do,
It's patriotic angels when there's outside work
　　to do.
We are not really senseless, and we are not
　　angels, too,
But very human beings, human just as much as
　　you.
It's hard upon occasions to be forceful and
　　sublime
When you're treated as incompetents three-
　　quarters of the time.
But it's women this and women that, and
　　woman's like a hen,
But it's do the country's work alone, when war
　　takes off the men,
And it's women this and women that and
　　everything you please,

But woman is observant, and be sure that
woman sees.

Those who wish to see the memory of the suffrage movement endure hope that women and men alike will continue
to see its significance and honor the labor that brought it to
fruition. They believe that if present-day Americans understand the different perspectives that shaped the movement,
they will better comprehend the social, political, and historical impact of universal suffrage. The ideal, however, will be
attained only when modern voters cherish and respect the
struggle that has enabled them to cast a ballot.

The Nineteenth Amendment gave women the right to vote but actually
benefits all U.S. voters.

Timeline

Late 1700s–early 1800s   While most American women occupy the domestic sphere, a few play a role in the abolitionist movement.

July 1848   Early suffrage advocates convene the Seneca Falls Convention to address the social status of American women; the convention issues the Declaration of Sentiments.

1866   Susan B. Anthony and other suffragists begin petitioning Congress to draft a constitutional amendment.

1869   Anthony and Elizabeth Cady Stanton form the National Woman Suffrage Association (NWSA); Lucy Stone, Henry Blackwell, and Julia Ward Howe organize the American Woman Suffrage Association (AWSA); Wyoming Territory becomes the first territory or state to extend suffrage to women.

1870   The Fifteenth Amendment, giving African-American men the right to vote, is ratified.

1890   NWSA and AWSA unite to form National American Woman Suffrage Association (NAWSA).

Late 1800s   Several western states and territories extend voting rights to women.

1900–1904   Carrie Chapman Catt serves her first term as president of NAWSA and establishes "suffrage schools," which instruct students in the background of the movement, in ways to bolster NAWSA membership, and in tactics for convincing all Americans that universal suffrage is in the nation's best interests.

1908   Theodore Roosevelt drafts a letter explaining his lukewarm support of American suffragists.

1910   Harriet Stanton Blatch forms the Women's Political Union (WPU).

March 13, 1913   Alice Paul organizes a NAWSA parade in Washington, D.C., that is timed to coincide with Woodrow Wilson's inauguration. Not long after this event, Paul and Lucy Burns form the Congressional Union for Woman Suffrage, which evolves into the National Woman's Party (NWP) by 1916.

September 7, 1916   Catt delivers a speech, "The Crisis," to a NAWSA convention in Atlantic City, New Jersey. Wilson, speaking at the same convention, begs suffragists for their continued patience.

1917   The Nebraska Association Opposed to Woman Suffrage (NAOWS) issues a pamphlet, *Ten Reasons Why the Great Majority of Women Do Not Want the Ballot*, arguing against giving women the vote.

January 1917   NWP members begin picketing the White House.

April 6, 1917   The United States formally enters World War I.

June 20, 1917   NWP activists picket the White House with banners that decry America for its lack of universal voting rights for women.

Summer 1917   Several prominent NWP members are jailed at Occoquan Workhouse, where they are force-fed and mistreated for their civil disobedience; they are released November 1918.

November 15, 1917   A night of abuse directed against suffragists at Occoquan Workhouse becomes known as the Night of Terror.

January 9, 1918   Wilson announces his support for the Nineteenth Amendment.

January 10, 1918   The U.S. House of Representatives votes overwhelmingly in favor of the Nineteenth Amendment.

Fall 1918   The U.S. Senate falls short of approving the Nineteenth Amendment by two votes.

June 1919   The U.S. Senate votes overwhelmingly in favor of releasing the Nineteenth Amendment for the states' ratification.

March 1920   By this date, thirty-five states have voted to ratify the Nineteenth Amendment.

August 18, 1920 Shortly after Tennessee's senate approves the Nineteenth Amendment, the state's house of representatives does the same.

August 24, 1920 Tennessee's governor, A. H. Roberts, issues a resolution that certifies his state's ratification of suffrage.

August 26, 1920 The Nineteenth Amendment, also referred to as the Susan B. Anthony Amendment, becomes part of the U.S. Constitution.

November 1920 Roughly one in three women in New York State votes in the presidential election, whereas two-thirds of men do.

1923 Alice Paul proposes the so-called equal rights amendment (ERA) at the seventy-fifth anniversary of the Seneca Falls Convention.

1960s The civil rights movement works to further racial equality and seeks voting reforms aimed at implementing the constitutional changes incorporated in the Fifteenth and Nineteenth amendments.

1963 Fannie Lou Hamer is imprisoned and beaten in Winona for attending a voter registration workshop; she subsequently becomes a founding member of the Mississippi Freedom Democratic Party (MFDP).

1964 The Twenty-fourth Amendment, eliminating the poll tax in federal elections, is ratified.

1965   The Voting Rights Act, which effectively prohibits literacy tests as a voter requirement, authorizes federal intervention in states and portions of states where a pattern of voting-rights abuses has been documented.

1971   Congress declares August 26 Women's Equality Day, in commemoration of the passage of the Nineteenth Amendment.

Fall 2008   Two female politicians, Hillary Clinton and Sarah Palin, run for office in a national election.

2009   As of this date, only five sovereign states — Lebanon, Brunei, Saudi Arabia, the United Arab Emirates, and Vatican City — continue to deny women the vote.

Notes

Chapter One

p. 11, ". . . a crisis has come to our movement . . . ": Social Justice Speeches: "The Crisis," EdChange Multicultural Pavilion, http://www.edchange.org/multicultural/speeches/catt_the_crisis.html (accessed November 24, 2008; date last updated not available).

p. 13, ". . . happen to have any learning . . . ": Gail Collins, "Toward the Revolutionary War," in *America's Women: Four Hundred Years of Dolls, Drudges, Helpmates, and Heroines*. New York: Morrow, 2003, p. 73.

p. 14, ". . . I suppose it will be necessary for you to make . . .": *Women of Influence: Abigail Smith Adams*, U.S. Department of State Publications, http://usinfo.state.gov/products/pubs/womeninfln/adams.htm (accessed November 24, 2008; date last updated not available).

p. 15, ". . . we find a full measure of duties . . .": "The Anti-Woman-Suffrage Movement," in *Appletons' Annual Cyclopaedia and Register of Important Events*. New York: D. Appleton, 1900, p. 15.

p. 18, ". . . these truths to be self-evident . . .": "The American Revolution: The Unfinished Revolution," May 13, 2003, National Park Service, http://www.nps.gov/revwar/unfinished_revolution/01_all_men_are_created_equal.html (accessed November 24, 2008).

p. 18, ". . . speak of woman as you do of the Negro . . .": "Women's Rights," in *Women's Words: The Columbia Book of Quotations by Women*, Mary Biggs, ed. New York: Columbia University Press, 1996, p. 454.

p. 20, ". . . stand outside the pale of . . .": "A Petition for Universal Suffrage," National Archives, http://www.archives.gov/global-pages/larger-image.html?i=/legislative/features/

suffrage/images/universal-suffrage-l.jpg&c=/legislative/ features/suffrage/images/universal-suffrage.caption.html (accessed June 23, 2009; date last updated not available).

p. 20, ". . . remaining class of disenfranchised . . .": "A Petition for Universal Suffrage," ibid.

p. 20, ". . . every state in the union . . .": "A Petition for Universal Suffrage," ibid.

p. 22, "destroy the home and family": "The Struggle for Women's Suffrage: Opponents of Suffrage," June 21, 2009,. Digital History, http://www.digitalhistory.uh.edu/database/article_ display.cfm?HHID=258 (accessed June 21, 2009).

p. 22, ". . . go your ways . . .": "Suffrage: Women's Right to Vote," Mark Twain Quotations, Newspaper Collections, and Related Resources, http://www.twainquotes.com/ Suffrage.html (Accessed June 21, 2009; date last updated not available).

p. 22, ". . . women transformed Wyoming from . . .": "Wyoming: The Equality State," Autry National Center of the American West, http://www.autrynationalcenter.org/explore/ exhibits/ suffrage/suffrage_wy.html (accessed June 21, 2009; date last updated not available).

p. 23, ". . . talk of sheltering woman . . .": Hearing of the Women Suffrage Association Before the House Committee on the Judiciary, January 18, 1892, December 3, 2007, Hanover College Department of History, http://history.hanover.edu/ courses/excerpts/111hear.html (accessed June 21, 2009).

Chapter Two

p. 25, ". . . with possibly ill-advised haste . . .": Sarah Hunter Graham, "A New Look for Suffrage," in *Woman Suffrage and the New Democracy*. New Haven, CT: Yale University Press, 1996, p. 22.

p. 25, ". . . with all their natural advantages . . .": Rosalyn Terborg-Penn, "Suffrage Strategies and Ideas," in *African American Women in the Struggle for the Vote, 1850–1920*. Bloomington: Indiana University Press, 1998, p. 60.

p. 28, ". . . are all the people?": "Marching for the Vote: Remembering the Woman Suffrage Parade of 1913," September 16, 2008, Library of Congress American Memory Project, http://lcweb2.loc.gov/ammem/awhhtml/aw01e/aw01e.html (accessed November 24, 2008).

p. 29, ". . . art and practice of government consists not . . .": Wilson's Address at the Woman Suffrage Convention, Atlantic City, N.J., September 8, 1916, in *President Wilson's State Papers and Addresses*. New York: Review of Reviews, 1918, p. 237.

p. 31, ". . . it is true that 'no woman capable . . .'": "No Time for Suffrage War," January 8, 1918, *New York Times*, http://query.nytimes.com/mem/archive-free/pdf?_r=2&res=9E01E EDB133FE433A2575AC0A9679C946996D6CF&oref=slo gin&oref=slogin (accessed November 24, 2008).

p. 32, "Silent Sentinels": "President Ignores Suffrage Pickets," January 10, 1917, *New York Times*, http://query.nytimes.com/mem/archive-free/pdf?res=990DE7DF1538EE32A25752C 1A9679C946696D6CF (accessed June 23, 2009).

p. 32, ". . . was utterly oblivious, apparently . . .": "President Ignores Suffrage Pickets," *New York Times*, http://query.nytimes.com/mem/archive-free/pdf?res=990DE7DF1538 EE32A25752C1A9679C946696D6CF (accessed June 23, 2009).

p. 33, ". . . tell you that America is not a democracy . . .": "Crowd Destroys Suffrage Banner at White House," June 20, 1917, *New York Times*, http://query.nytimes.com/mem/

archive-free/pdf?res=9907E0D9123BE03ABC4951DFB0
66838C609EDE (accessed November 24, 2008).

p. 33, ". . . another banner with the same wording . . .": "Crowd
Destroys Suffrage Banner at White House," June 20, 1917,
New York Times, http://query.nytimes.com/mem/archive-free
/pdf?res=9907E0D9123BE03ABC4951DFB066838C609
EDE (accessed November 24, 2008).

p. 33, ". . . was injurious to the suffrage . . .": "Crowd Destroys
Suffrage Banner at White House," June 20, 1917, *New York
Times*, http://query.nytimes.com/mem/archive-free/pdf?r
es=9907E0D9123BE03ABC4951DFB066838C609EDE
(accessed November 24, 2008).

p. 33, ". . . not in any way in sympathy with . . .": "Crowds
Again Rend Suffrage Banners," June 21, 1917, *New York
Times*, http://query.nytimes.com/mem/archive-free/pdf?_r=
1&res=9B03E3D8123BE03ABC4A51DFB066838C609E
DE (accessed June 21, 2009).

Chapter Three

p. 34, ". . . believe in women's suffrage . . .": "Prominent
Americans and Woman Suffrage," May 22, 2006, Library
of Congress: American Memory Project, http://memory.loc.
gov/learn/collections/miller/history3.html (accessed June
22, 2009).

p. 37, ". . . they have not lost faith . . .": "Woman Suffrage,"
Nebraska State Historical Society. http://www.
nebraskahistory.org/publish/publicat/timeline/woman_
suffrage.htm (accessed June 22, 2009).

p. 39, ". . . that we have to give our sons to the service of the
country . . .": "Crowd Destroys Suffrage Banner at White
House," June 20, 1917, *New York Times*, http://query.
nytimes.com/mem/archive-free/pdf?res=9907E0D9123BE

03ABC4951DFB066838C609EDE (accessed November 24, 2008).

p. 39, ". . . you take that banner . . .": "Crowd Destroys Suffrage Banner at White House," June 20, 1917, *New York Times*, http://query.nytimes.com/mem/archive-free/pdf?res=9907E0D9123BE03ABC4951DFB066838C609EDE (accessed November 24, 2008).

p. 39, "outrage": "Crowd Destroys Suffrage Banner at White House," June 20, 1917, *New York Times*, http://query.nytimes.com/mem/archive-free/pdf?res=9907E0D9123BE03ABC4951DFB066838C609EDE (accessed November 24, 2008).

p. 39, "treason": "Crowd Destroys Suffrage Banner at White House," June 20, 1917, *New York Times*, http://query.nytimes.com/mem/archive-free/pdf?res=9907E0D9123BE03ABC4951DFB066838C609EDE (accessed November 24, 2008).

p. 40, ". . . who believes in the principle of . . .": "Crowd Destroys Suffrage Banner at White House," June 20, 1917, *New York Times*, http://query.nytimes.com/mem/archive-free/pdf?res=9907E0D9123BE03ABC4951DFB066838C609EDE (accessed November 24, 2008).

p. 41, ". . . have we come to in . . .": "Arrest Forty-One Pickets for Suffrage at the White House," November 11, 1917, *New York Times*, http://query.nytimes.com/gst/abstract.html?res=9F03EFD8123FE433A25752C1A9679D946696D6CF (accessed June 23, 2009).

p. 42, ". . . thrust into cells; the ventilators were . . .": Inez Haynes Irwin, "The Strange Ladies," in *The Story of the Woman's Party*. New York: Harcourt, Brace, 1921, p. 375.

p. 44, ". . . time that the sportsmanship and gallantry . . .": "White House Pickets Held without Bail," November

13, 1917, *New York Times*, http://query.nytimes.com/mem
/archive-free/pdf?_r=1&res=9D07E7DF133FE433A25757
C1A9679D946696D6C (accessed June 22, 2009).

p. 44, ". . . facts represent an intolerable condition . . .": "Move
Militants from Workhouse," November 24, 1917, *New York
Times*, http://query.nytimes.com/mem/archive-free/pdf?re
s=9A06E5D7113AE433A25756C2A9679D946696D6CF
(accessed June 22, 2009).

Chapter Four

p. 48, ". . . had not felt at liberty . . .": Katherine H. Adams and
Michael L. Keene, "Hunger Strikes and Jail," in *Alice Paul
and the American Suffrage Campaign*. Urbana: University of
Illinois Press, 2008, p. 213.

p. 49, ". . . express our gratification at the president's stand
. . .": "Wilson Backs Amendment for Woman Suffrage,"
January 9, 1918, *New York Times*, http://query.nytimes.
com/mem/archive-free/pdf?_r=1&res=9803E5DA133FE4
33A25753C1A9679C946996D6CF&oref=slogin (accessed
November 24, 2008).

p. 50, ". . . our president, the great leader. . ." "Wilson Backs
Amendment for Woman Suffrage," http://query.nytimes.
com/mem/archive-free/pdf?_r=1&res=9803E5DA133FE4
33A25753C1A9679C946996D6CF&oref=slogin (accessed
November 24, 2008).

p. 50, ". . . citizens of the United States to vote . . .": Transcript
of Nineteenth Amendment to the U.S. Constitution:
Women's Right to Vote (1920), Our Documents: One
Hundred Milestone Documents from the National
Archives, http://www.ourdocuments.gov/doc.php?flash=
true&doc=63&page=transcript (accessed November 24,
2008; date last updated not available).

p. 51, ". . . cast upon this amendment would deprive any . . .": Modern History Sourcebook: The Passage of the Nineteenth Amendment, 1919–1920 (articles from the *New York Times*), September 1997, Fordham University, http://www.fordham. edu/halsall/mod/1920womensvote.html (accessed November 24, 2008; date last updated not available).

p. 52, ". . . made partners of the women in this . . .": "September 30, 1918: A Vote for Women," U.S. Senate, Historical Minute Essays: 1878–1920, http://senate.gov/artandhistory/history/minute/A_Vote_For_Women.htm (accessed November 24, 2008; date last updated not available).

p. 53, ". . . the question is . . .": Modern History Sourcebook: The Passage of the Nineteenth Amendment, 1919–1920, http://www.fordham.edu/halsall/mod/1920womensvote. html (accessed November 24, 2008; date last updated not available).

p. 54, ". . . last stage of the fight is to obtain . . .": Modern History Sourcebook: The Passage of the Nineteenth Amendment, 1919–1920 (articles from the *New York Times*), September 1997, Fordham University, http://www.fordham.edu/halsall/mod/1920womensvote.html (accessed November 24, 2008; date last updated not available).

p. 55, ". . . battle has been fought and won . . .": "'Don't Forget to Be a Good Boy': Harry T. Burn's Letter from Mom and the Ratification of the Nineteenth Amendment in Tennessee," Teaching American History, http://www.teachamericanhistory.org/File/Harry_T._Burn.pdf (accessed June 22, 2009; date last updated not available).

p. 56, ". . . women moved along the curb . . .": Modern History Sourcebook: The Passage of the Nineteenth Amendment, 1919–1920, http://www.teachamericanhistory.org/File/Harry

_T._Burn.pdf (accessed June 22, 2009; date last updated not available).

p. 58, ". . . a mother's advice is always safest . . .": Gail Collins, "Reforming the World," in *America's Women: Four Hundred Years of Dolls, Drudges, Helpmates, and Heroines*. New York: Morrow, 2003, p. 314.

Chapter Five

p. 60, ". . . the first test of universal suffrage . . .": "One in Three Women Vote," December 19, 1920, *New York Times*, http://query.nytimes.com/mem/archive-free/pdf?_r=1&res=990DEED9103FE432A2575AC1A9649D946195D6CF&oref=slogi (accessed November 24, 2008).

p. 61, ". . . came to women in many states too late . . .": "One in Three Women Vote," http://query.nytimes.com/mem/archive-free/pdf?_r=1&res=990DEED9103FE432A2575AC1A9649D946195D6CF&oref=slogi (accessed November 24, 2008).

p. 61, ". . . I know refrained from voting . . .": "One in Three Women Vote," http://query.nytimes.com/mem/archive-free/pdf?_r=1&res=990DEED9103FE432A2575AC1A9649D946195D6CF&oref=slogi (accessed November 24, 2008).

p. 63, ". . . newly come into the possession of . . .": "Fooling Women Voters," September 20, 1920, *New York Times*, http://query.nytimes.com/mem/archive-free/pdf?res=9A04E1DC1F31E433A25755C2A96F9C946195D6CF (accessed November 24, 2008).

p. 64, ". . . women shall have equal rights . . .": "The History behind the Equal Rights Amendment," September 1, 2008, The Equal Rights Amendment, http://www.equalrightsamendment.org/era.htm (accessed November 24, 2008).

p. 65, ". . . rights under the law shall not be denied . . .": "The Equal Rights Amendment," National Organization for Women, http://www.now.org/issues/economic/eratext.html (accessed November 24, 2008; date last updated not available).

p. 66, ". . . Freedom Democratic Party isn't seated . . .": "Fannie Lou Hamer Quotes," Repaying Our Ancestors Respectfully (ROAR): Fannie Lou Hamer, http://www.fannielouhamer. info/ (accessed June 22, 2009; date last updated not available).

p. 68, ". . . is not a 'right' . . .": Susan Youngblood Ashmore, "Wallace's Infrastructure," in *Carry It On: The War on Poverty and the Civil Rights Movement in Alabama, 1964–1972*. Athens: University of Georgia Press, 2008, p. 91.

p. 69, ". . . seek to avoid action . . .": Presidential Libraries: History Uncovered—Johnson, C-SPAN, http://www.c-span.org/PresidentialLibraries/Content/LBJ/LBJ_VotingRights.pdf (accessed November 24, 2008; date last updated not available),

p. 70, ". . . are still countries that do not recognize . . .": Interview with Kris Myers, director of Heritage and Outreach at the Alice Paul Institute, November 18, 2008.

p. 71, ". . . have so little interaction . . .": "Saudi Government Bans Women's Suffrage," October 11, 2004, MSNBC, http://www.msnbc.msn.com/id/6228405/) (accessed June 22, 2009).

p. 71, ". . . the point of voting . . .": "Saudi Government Bans Women's Suffrage," http://www.msnbc.msn.com/id/6228405/) (accessed June 22, 2009).

p. 72, ". . . are capable of voting and making the right . . .": "Saudi Government Bans Women's Suffrage," http://www.msnbc.msn.com/id/6228405/) (accessed June 22, 2009).

p. 72, ". . . working to lobby for women . . .": "Saudi Arabia: Women without the Vote," September 4, 2008, International Museum of Women: Women, Power, and Politics. http://www.imow.org/wpp/stories/viewStory? storyId=1622 (accessed June 22, 2009).

Chapter Six

p. 75, ". . . would look at voting merely as a right . . .": Interview with Laura Piché, graduate student and American voter, May 23, 2009.

p. 75, ". . . voting to be the right *and* the obligation . . .": Interview with Pat Spilseth, writer and American voter, November 18, 2008.

p. 76, ". . . heroes Americans celebrate are . . .": Interview with Kris Myers, November 18, 2008.

p. 77, ". . .when people hear the phrase . . .": Interview with Kris Myers, November 18, 2008.

p. 78, ". . . would hope more people would vote . . .": Interview with Melissa Kennedy, librarian and American voter, November 1, 2008.

p. 78, ". . . younger generation is often blamed . . .": Interview with Kris Myers, November 18, 2008.

p. 80, ". . . the women of the United States have been treated . . .": "What Is Women's Equality Day?" National Women's History Project (NWHP), http://www.nwhp.org/resource center/equalityday.php (accessed June 22, 2009; date last updated not available).

p. 82, ". . . to ask my government if they would set me free . . .": Alice Duer Miller, "Women," in *Are Women People: A Book of Rhymes for Suffrage Times*. New York: Doran, 1915, p. 74.

Further Information

Books

Marsico, Katie. *Woodrow Wilson*. New York: Marshall Cavendish, 2010.

McPherson, Stephanie Sammartino. *Susan B. Anthony*. Minne-
apolis: Lerner, 2006.

Mountjoy, Shane. *The Women's Rights Movement: Moving toward
Equality*. New York: Chelsea House, 2008.

Van Meter, Larry A. *Women Win the Vote: The Hard-Fought
Battle for Women's Suffrage*. Berkeley Heights, NJ: Enslow,
2009.

DVDs

Iron Jawed Angels. Directed by Katja von Garnier; Hillary
Swank, Julia Ormond, Anjelica Huston. 2004. HBO Home
Video, 2004.

*Not for Ourselves Alone: The Story of Elizabeth Cady Stanton and
Susan B. Anthony*. Directed by Ken Burns; Sally Kellerman,
Ronnie Gilbert, Julie Harris. 2004. PBS Paramount,
1999.

Websites

Alice Paul Institute

www.alicepaul.org/

A website that contains detailed information about Paul, her
suffrage efforts, and her legacy in the twenty-first century.

Fordham University — Modern History Sourcebook: The Passage of the Nineteenth Amendment, 1919–1920
www.fordham.edu/halsall/mod/1920womensvote.html
A comprehensive site with a collection of *New York Times* articles related to the passage of the Nineteenth Amendment.

Our Documents: One Hundred Documents from the National Archives — Transcript of Nineteenth Amendment to the U.S. Constitution: Women's Right to Vote (1920)
www.ourdocuments.gov/doc.php?flash=true&doc=63&page=transcript
A website featuring a photographic copy and accompanying explanation of the Nineteenth Amendment.

Bibliography

Books

Adams, Katherine H., and Michael L. Keene. *Alice Paul and the American Suffrage Campaign.* Urbana: University of Illinois Press, 2008.

Appletons' Annual Cyclopaedia and Register of Important Events. New York: Appleton, 1900.

Ashmore, Susan Youngblood. *Carry It On: The War on Poverty and the Civil Rights Movement in Alabama, 1964–1972.* Athens: University of Georgia Press, 2008.

Biggs, Mary, ed. *Women's Words: The Columbia Book of Quotations by Women.* New York: Columbia University Press, 1996.

Braden, Maria. *Women Politicians and the Media.* Lexington: University Press of Kentucky, 1996.

Buhle, Mari Jo, and Paul Buhle, eds. *The Concise History of Woman Suffrage.* Urbana: University of Illinois Press, 1978.

Catt, Carrie Chapman, and Nettie Rogers Shuler. *Woman Suffrage and Politics.* Seattle: University of Washington Press, 1923.

Collins, Gail. *America's Women: Four Hundred Years of Dolls, Drudges, Helpmates, and Heroines.* New York: Morrow, 2003.

DuBois, Ellen, and Richard Cándida Smith, eds. *Elizabeth Cady Stanton, Feminist as Thinker: A Reader in Documents and Essays.* New York: New York University Press, 2007.

Graham, Sarah Hunter. *Woman Suffrage and the New Democracy.* New Haven, CT: Yale University Press, 1996.

Hill, Jeff. *Defining Moments: Women's Suffrage*. Detroit: Omnigraphics, 2006.

Irwin, Inez Haynes. *The Story of the Woman's Party*. New York: Harcourt, Brace, 1921.

Miller, Alice Duer. *Are Women People: A Book of Rhymes for Suffrage Times*. New York: Doran, 1915.

President Wilson's State Papers and Addresses. New York: Review of Reviews, 1918.

Terborg-Penn, Rosalyn. *African American Women in the Struggle for the Vote, 1850–1920*. Bloomington: Indiana University Press, 1998.

Interviews

With Melissa Kennedy, librarian and American voter, November 1, 2008.

With Ann Konrath, retiree and American voter, November 10, 2008.

With Kris Myers, director of Heritage and Outreach at the Alice Paul Institute, November 18, 2008.

With Laura Piché, graduate student and American voter, May 23, 2009.

With Pat Spilseth, writer and American voter, November 18, 2008.

Websites

Alice Paul Institute
www.alicepaul.org/

Autry National Center of the American West—Wyoming: The Equality State
www.autrynationalcenter.org/explore/exhibits/suffrage/suffrage_wy.html

C-SPAN—Presidential Libraries: History Uncovered—Johnson
www.c-span.org/PresidentialLibraries/Content/LBJ/LBJ_VotingRights.pdf

Digital History—The Struggle for Women's Suffrage: Opponents of Suffrage
www.digitalhistory.uh.edu/database/article_display.cfm?HHID=258

EdChange Multicultural Pavilion—Social Justice Speeches: "The Crisis" www.edchange.org/multicultural/speeches/ catt_the_crisis.html

Fordham University—Modern History Sourcebook: The Passage of the Nineteenth Amendment, 1919–1920 (articles from the *New York Times*)
www.fordham.edu/halsall/mod/1920womensvote.html

Hanover College, Department of History: Hearing of the Women Suffrage Association before the House Committee on the Judiciary, January 18, 1892
www.history.hanover.edu/courses/excerpts/111hear.html

International Museum of Women—Women, Power, and Politics: "Saudi Arabia: Women without the Vote"
www.imow.org/wpp/stories/viewStory?storyId=1622

League of Women Voters—About Us
www.lwv.org/AM/Template.cfm?Section=About_Us

Library of Congress American Memory Project—Marching
for the Vote: Remembering the Woman Suffrage Parade of
1913
www.lcweb2.loc.gov/ammem/awhhtml/aw01e/aw01e.html

Library of Congress American Memory Project—Prominent
Americans and Woman Suffrage
www.memory.loc.gov/learn/collections/miller/history3.html

Mark Twain Quotations, Newspaper Collections, and Related Resources—Suffrage: Women's Right to Vote
www.twainquotes.com/Suffrage.html

MSNBC—"Saudi Government Bans Women's Suffrage"
www.msnbc.msn.com/id/6228405/)

National Archives—A Petition for Universal Suffrage
www.archives.gov/global-pages/larger-image.html?i=/
legislative/features/suffrage/images/universal-suffrage-l.
jpg&c=/legislative/features/suffrage/images/universal-
suffrage.caption.html

National Park Service—The American Revolution: The
Unfinished Revolution
www.nps.gov/revwar/unfinished_revolution/01_all_men_
are_created_equal.html

National Women's History Project—What Is Women's
Equality Day?
www.nwhp.org/resourcecenter/equalityday.php

Nebraska State Historical Society—Woman Suffrage
www.nebraskahistory.org/publish/publicat/timeline/
woman_suffrage.htm

Newsweek—"From Seneca Falls to Sarah Palin?"
www.newsweek.com/id/158893

New York Times, "Arrest Forty-One Pickets for Suffrage at
the White House"
http://query.nytimes.com/gst/abstract.html?res=9F03EFD8
123FE433A25752C1A9679D946696D6CF

New York Times, "Crowd Destroys Suffrage Banner at White
House"
http://query.nytimes.com/mem/archive-free/pdf?res=9907E
0D9123BE03ABC4951DFB066838C609EDE

New York Times, "Crowds Again Rend Suffrage Banners"
http://query.nytimes.com/mem/archive-free/pdf?_r=1&res=
9B03E3D8123BE03ABC4A51DFB066838C609EDE

New York Times, "Fooling Women Voters"
http://query.nytimes.com/mem/archive-free/pdf?res=9A04E
1DC1F31E433A25755C2A96F9C946195D6CF

New York Times, "Move Militants from Workhouse"
http://query.nytimes.com/mem/archive-free/pdf?res=9A06E
5D7113AE433A25756C2A9679D946696D6CF

New York Times, "No Time for Suffrage War"
http://query.nytimes.com/mem/archive-free/pdf?_r=2&res=
9E01EEDB133FE433A2575AC0A9679C946996D6CF&or
ef=slogin&oref=slogin

New York Times, "One in Three Women Vote"
http://query.nytimes.com/mem/archive-free/pdf?_r=1&res=
990DEED9103FE432A2575AC1A9649D946195D6CF&o
ref=slogi

New York Times, "President Ignores Suffrage Pickets"
http://query.nytimes.com/mem/archive-free/pdf?res=990DE
7DF1538EE32A25752C1A9679C946696D6CF

New York Times, "White House Pickets Held without Bail"
http://query.nytimes.com/mem/archive-free/pdf?_r=1&res=
9D07E7DF133FE433A25757C1A9679D946696D6C

New York Times, "Wilson Backs Amendment for Woman
Suffrage"
http://query.nytimes.com/mem/archive-free/pdf?_r=1&res=
9803E5DA133FE433A25753C1A9679C946996D6CF&ore
f=slogin

Our Documents: One Hundred Documents from the
National Archives—Transcript of Nineteenth Amendment
to the U.S. Constitution: Women's Right to Vote (1920)
www.ourdocuments.gov/doc.php?flash=true&doc=63&page
=transcript

Repaying Our Ancestors Respectfully (ROAR): Fannie Lou
Hamer Quotes
www.fannielouhamer.info/

Teaching American History—"Don't Forget to Be a Good
Boy": Harry T. Burn's Letter from Mom and the Ratification
of the Nineteenth Amendment in Tennessee
www.teachamericanhistory.org/File/Harry_T._Burn.pdf

U.S. Department of State: Publications—Women of Influence: Abigail Smith Adams
http://usinfo.state.gov/products/pubs/womeninfln/adams.htm

U.S. Senate: Historical Women Essays—1878–1920, September 30, 1918, a Vote for Women
http://Senate.gov/artandhistory/history/minute/A_Vote_For_Women.htm

Index

Page numbers in **boldface** are illustrations.

About the Author

KATIE MARSICO is the author of more than sixty reference books for children and young adults. Prior to becoming a full-time writer, Ms. Marsico worked as a managing editor in publishing. She resides near Chicago, Illinois, with her husband and three children.